Farmer Neal & His Wheat Field

Monica Stephenson

Archway Publishing
1663 Liberty Drive
Bloomington, IN 47403
www.archwaypublishing.com
844-669-3957

Interior Image Credit: Nikkie Stephenson

ISBN: 978-1-6657-1379-5 (sc)
ISBN: 978-1-6657-1378-8 (hc)
ISBN: 978-1-6657-1380-1 (e)

Archway Publishing rev. date: 11/04/2021

Farmer Neal & His Wheat Field

Today in Nealville...
It's a warm and sunny day in September. Farmer Neal is getting ready to plant his wheat crop. He has his big tractor all fueled up and ready to go!

Turner Seed Compa

First, Farmer Neal must go to town and buy some wheat seed from Darcy. Darcy owns a seed company where you can buy any kind of seed you want to plant.

Farmer Neal gets his truck out of the barn and takes it to Darcy's seed store and fills it with wheat seed.

On the way back from town, Farmer Neal passes another farmer in his field preparing to plant his wheat crop.

He gives a big wave out the window as he drives by.

Once Farmer Neal arrives back to the field, he augers the grain from his truck into the planter.

Farmer Neal heads to the field to plant his wheat. Around and around the field he goes.

Looking off into the distance, Farmer Neal sees a rain cloud. He hurries to get his wheat planted before the storm.

No sooner than Farmer Neal gets done, the gentle rain starts to fall. Farmer Neal smiles. He knows in a few days the wheat seed will sprout.

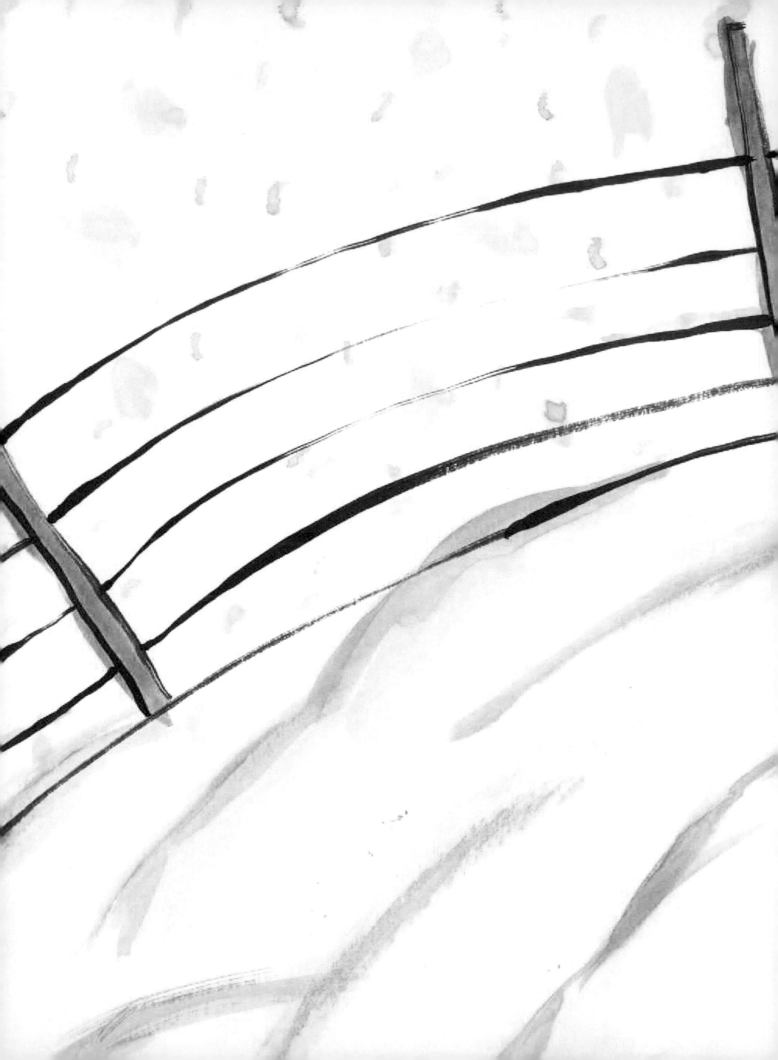

Farmer Neal watches his wheat crop grow all winter through the cold and snowy days.

Finally, it's spring! The wheat heads start popping up. Soon, Farmer Neal will be able to harvest his crops.

The days get longer and hotter.

One sunny day in June, Farmer Neal gets his combine out of the barn and prepares it for the wheat harvest.

Farmer Neal cuts the wheat with his combine, loads his truck full of wheat, and heads to the grain elevator in town.

After he unloads his truck, he heads back to the farm to prepare his fields for planting the next crop.

Printed in the United States
by Baker & Taylor Publisher Services